Grandpa and Me

by Heidi Pross Gray

Written and illustrated for my incredibly talented, most amazing Gramma. I am forever grateful for our summers together, circumstances aside, and I thank God every day for having you in my life. I love you super mega bunches forever and ever!

We're visiting Gramma
And Grandpa today!
They are so much fun
And they love to play.

First we play
cards
Or read a book,

Then off to the
kitchen
To help Gramma
cook!

Out on the deck
We gaze into the trees.
Look! A hummingbird
Darts through the leaves.

The warm sweet air
Calls our name.
No two of our hikes
Are ever the same.

What will we see?
Where will we go?
Each trek's an
adventure
There's no
way
to know!

We pack our bags. Don't forget lunch!
And a hat and a crayon or maybe a bunch.

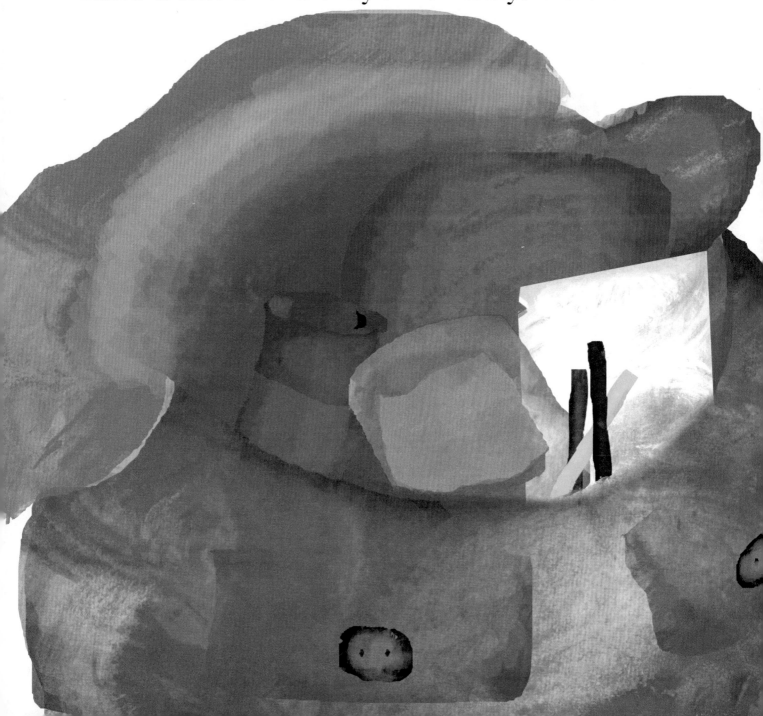

Bursting with joy
So excited are we.
We're off on our hike
Just Grandpa and me.

Down through the woods, the path is so narrow.
What shall we see? A tulip or sparrow?

Look over here!
By the roots of the tree
Five mushrooms are growing.
Count them with me!

The warblers are singing
I hear them exclaim,
"Look up in the trees!"
Two calling my name.

Around the boulder
And up the small hill.
Four chipmunks
scurry.
They never stay still!

Off to the right
Is the green swamp so grand.
Kept by a beaver-
The best builder on land!

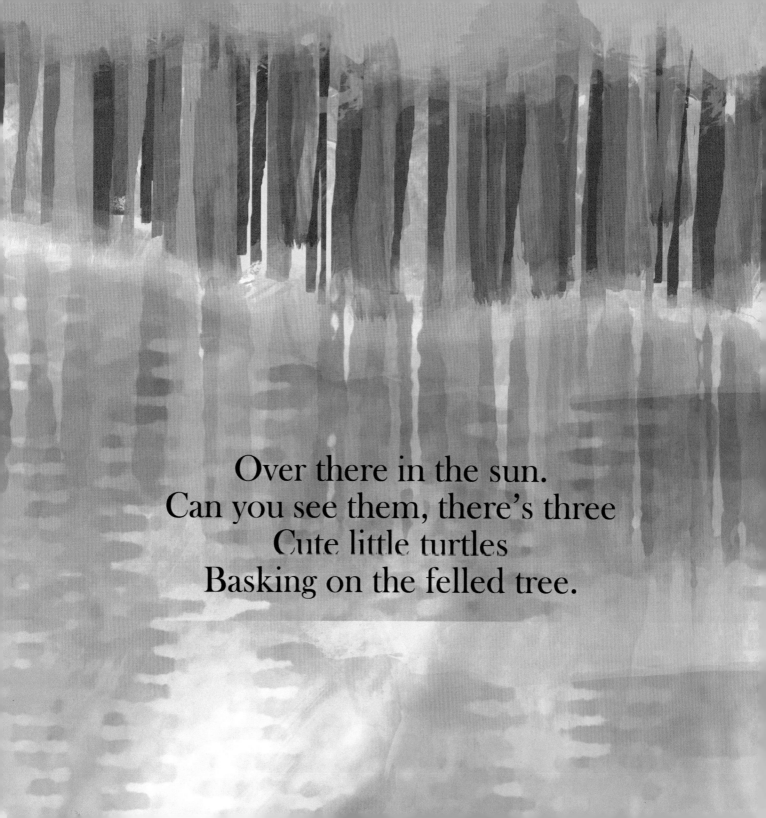

Over there in the sun.
Can you see them, there's three
Cute little turtles
Basking on the felled tree.

There's a break in the trees.
Grandpa points out to me
One bald eagle soaring
So majestic, so free.

Climbing higher and higher
Up the mountain we go.
I see Gramma's house
So small down below.

Whatever it is
I hope it doesn't attack!

We're getting hungry.
Here's a nice spot
To take a quick break,
Eat the lunch that we brought.

And now we gaze into the sky so blue...

Six cotton ball clouds are just passing through.

I take the last bite
And lick off my thumbs
While seven hungry ants
March off with the crumbs.

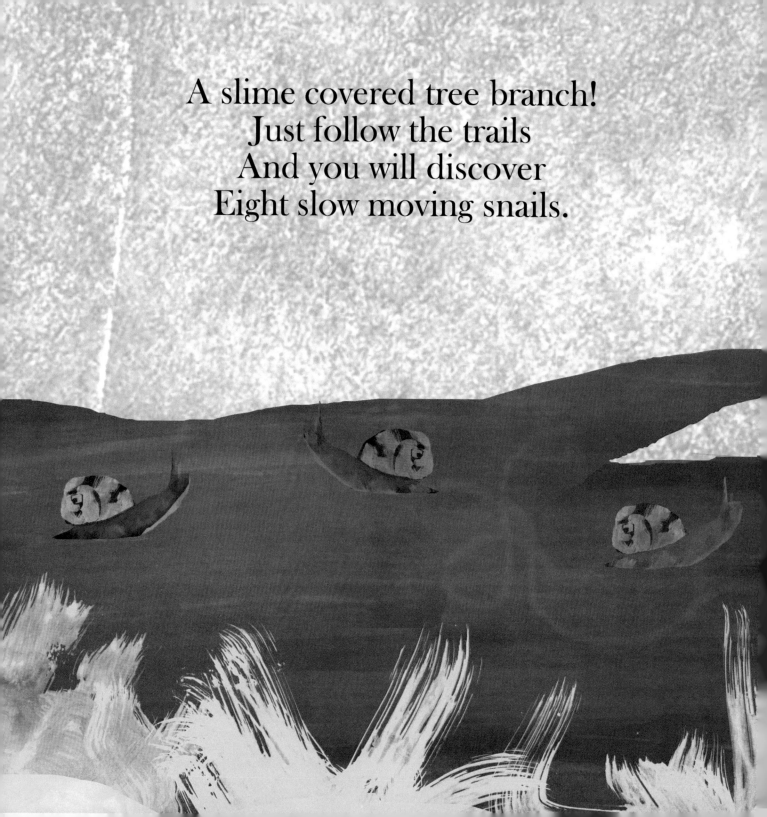

A slime covered tree branch!
Just follow the trails
And you will discover
Eight slow moving snails.

The forest is speckled
With big rocks and boulders.
Can you believe it? They stand
Higher than my shoulders!

It's like a huge
mountain,
A fortress of might.

Scramble to the top
Nine boulders in sight.

Down through the valley
Calm meadows so green,

Ten deer are grazing
Peaceful and serene.

Back home to Gramma.
We are on our way.
We saw so many things.
What a special fun day.

There's so much we learned
And much more to see.
I love our afternoon hikes
Just Grandpa and me.

About <u>Grandpa and Me</u>

Grandpa and Me is based on the real life memories that the author, Heidi, has from visiting her Gramma and Grandpa in a rural part of northern New Jersey. It is a beautiful part of the country filled with all sorts of wildlife, trees, birds, and it truly is an adventure every time one goes outside. It is quite common to see raccoons and bears in this part of the country (though we try to stay inside when we see them which is why they weren't in this book!) as well as deer and the other animals you read about in Grandpa and Me. Even the beaver in this story is based on a real beaver that created a small swamp just outside of Heidi's grandparents' backyard. One winter, the swampy lake froze over and Heidi and her cousins went ice skating on it!

The next time you are with your parent or grandparent, take them outside and go for a nature walk! You might not live near the woods, but there is nature everywhere, from the desert to the beach and everywhere in between. Take notes about what you see, draw pictures, and share them with your family. And most of all, make memories exploring outside together!

About the Author

Heidi is a mother of four and loves the outdoors! She has lived in a variety of climates and terrain, but really finds something special in the woods because of the fond memories of her childhood exploring with her grandfather and father!

Want to read more of Heidi's books? Collect all of Heidi's books about the seasons!

Autumn is Here
Winter is Here
Spring is Here
Summer is Here

To learn more about Heidi, purchase books, and to visit her Montessori toy store, come to Cake in the Morn at www.cakeinthemorn.com.